Animal World

Animal Sizes

Patricia Whitehouse

Raintree

www.raintreepublishers.co.uk

Visit our website to find out more information about **Raintree** books.

To order:
☎ Phone 44 (0) 1865 888112
🗎 Send a fax to 44 (0) 1865 314091
💻 Visit the Raintree Bookshop at **raintreepublishers.co.uk** to browse our catalogue and order online.

First published in Great Britain by Raintree, Halley Court, Jordan Hill, Oxford OX2 8EJ, part of Harcourt Education.
Raintree is a registered trademark of Harcourt Education Ltd.

Editorial: Nick Hunter and Diyan Leake
Design: Sue Emerson (HL-US) and Michelle Lisseter
Picture Research: Amor Montes de Oca (HL-US) and Maria Joannou
Production: Lorraine Hicks

Originated by Dot Gradations
Printed and bound in China by South China Printing Company

ISBN 1 844 21538 5
07 06 05 04 03
10 9 8 7 6 5 4 3 2 1

British Library Cataloguing in Publication Data
Whitehouse, Patricia
Animal Sizes
516.1'5
A full catalogue record for this book is available from the British Library.

Acknowledgements
The publishers would like to thank the following for permission to reproduce photographs: A. B. Sheldon pp. 14 (crocodile), 17 (gorilla); Bruce Coleman, Inc./Norman Owen Tomalin pp. 16 (kangaroo), 17 (chimpanzee), 19 (ostrich) ; Byron Jorjorian p. 18 (camel); Corbis p. 5 (giraffe, W. Wayne Lockwood, M.D.); Dwight Kuhn pp. 4 (gecko), 10, 12 (gecko), 13 (puffin), back cover (puffin); E. R. Degginger pp. 4 (wallaby), 16 (wallaby); FLPA p. 22; Impeccable Images p. 20 (Lew and Marti Ligocki); Index Stock Imagery p. 18 (giraffe, Michael Long); James P. Rowan pp. 4 (elephant), 7, 8, 9, 11, 12 (spider monkey), 22, back cover (rhinoceros); Minden Pictures pp. 5 (hippopotamus, Gerry Ellis), 6 (Jim Brandenburg), 13 (penguin, Frans Lanting), 14 (iguana, Claus Meyer), 19 (flamingo, Tui De Roy); NHPA pp. 15 (grass snake), 23; Visuals Unlimited p. 15 (python, Joe McDonald), 21 (sea lion, Milton H. Tierney)

Cover photograph of a cattle egret on a hippopotamus, reproduced with permission of NHPA

Contents

What sizes do animals come in?

wallaby

elephant

 gecko

Animals come in many sizes.

giraffe

hippopotamus

Some animals are tall.

Some animals are big.

Some animals are small.

Are these animals big or small?

trunk

An elephant is a big animal.

It has big ears and a big trunk.

A hippopotamus is a big animal.

It has a big body and a big head.

Which animal is bigger?

elephant

hippopotamus

Some big animals are bigger than others.

The elephant is bigger than the hippopotamus.

rhinoceros

polar bear

The rhinoceros is bigger than the polar bear.

Are these animals big or small?

A gecko is a small animal.

It has small eyes and small feet.

A spider monkey is a small animal.

It has a small head and a
small body.

Which animal is smaller?

gecko

spider monkey

Some small animals are smaller than others.

The gecko is smaller than the spider monkey.

penguin

puffin

A puffin is smaller than a penguin.

Which animal is longer?

crocodile

iguana

Crocodiles have long bodies and long tails.

A crocodile is longer than an iguana.

python

baby grass snake

Snakes have long bodies.

A python is longer than
a grass snake.

Which animal is shorter?

wallaby

kangaroo

Wallabies have short bodies.

A wallaby is shorter than a kangaroo.

gorilla

chimpanzee

A chimpanzee is shorter than a gorilla.

Which animal is taller?

giraffe

camel

A giraffe's long neck and long legs make it tall.

A giraffe is taller than a camel.

ostrich

flamingo

An ostrich is taller than a flamingo.

How big are baby animals?

Baby animals are not as big as their mothers.

The mother giraffe is taller than her baby.

The mother sea lion is longer than her baby.

How do baby animals change?

lion cub

lioness

Baby animals may look like their parents.

When they are babies, they are very small.

Baby animals do not stay small.

They grow until they are as big as their parents.

Index

24

Titles in the Animal World series include:

Hardback   1 844 21535 0

Hardback   1 844 21536 9

Hardback   1 844 21537 7

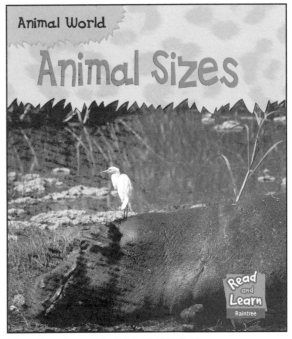

Hardback   1 844 21538 5

Find out about the other titles in this series on our website www.heinemann.co.uk/library